THE BOOK ON RENTAL PROPERTY INVESTING

Guide on How to Create Wealth Successful With Rental Property Investing

Henry Winfrey

Copyright

Disclaimer

This book is designed to provide condensed information. It's not intended to reprint all the information that is otherwise available, but instead to complement, amplify and supplement other texts. You are urged to read all available materials, learn as much as possible and tailor the information to your individual needs.

The purpose of this book is to educate.

TABLE OF CONTENT

INTRODUCTION

In the bustling city of Cascade, Emily Turner embarked on a journey that transformed her life through rental property investing. Armed with a passion for real estate and a keen eye for opportunity, Emily began her venture with a modest duplex in a growing neighborhood.

Her initial challenges were met with determination as she tirelessly researched market trends and local dynamics. Emily's dedication to understanding the nuances of the real estate market allowed her to make informed decisions, turning her duplex into a profitable investment. She quickly learned the importance of location, choosing neighborhoods with high demand and potential for growth.

As Emily's portfolio expanded, so did her financial acumen. She meticulously managed her budget, explored diverse financing options, and leveraged her resources to acquire more properties. Each investment was a calculated move, contributing to her steadily increasing cash flow.

Tenant management became a key aspect of Emily's success. Through thorough screening processes, she attracted reliable tenants and fostered positive landlord-tenant relationships. Emily understood the significance of maintaining well-kept properties, promptly addressing maintenance issues, and ensuring tenant satisfaction, which ultimately resulted in lower turnover rates.

One of Emily's defining moments came when she navigated legal and tax complexities associated with rental property ownership. With a proactive approach, she stayed informed about landlord-tenant laws and optimized her tax strategies, maximizing her returns while minimizing risks.

As Emily's success story unfolded, she became an inspiration to aspiring investors in Cascade. She openly shared her experiences, offering valuable insights and advice to those eager to follow in her footsteps. Emily's commitment to ongoing education, coupled with adaptability to market trends, allowed her to stay ahead of the curve.

Over the years, Emily's rental property investments not only provided financial stability but also afforded her the freedom to pursue other passions. Her story serves as a testament to the transformative power of strategic rental property investing, proving that with dedication, knowledge, and resilience, anyone can turn a humble beginning into a thriving real estate portfolio.

Welcome to "The Book on Rental Property Investing," a comprehensive guide designed to unlock the doors to financial success through the dynamic world of real estate. Whether you're a seasoned investor seeking to optimize your portfolio or a novice eager to embark on your first venture, this book is your roadmap to navigating the complexities of rental property investment.

In the pages that follow, we will delve into the fundamentals of rental property investing, exploring key strategies, insightful case studies, and practical tips that have empowered individuals to build wealth and secure a brighter financial future. From understanding market dynamics to mastering property management and maximizing rental income, each chapter is crafted to equip you with the knowledge and skills essential for success in the competitive real estate landscape.

The journey begins with a holistic approach, emphasizing the importance of thorough research, strategic planning, and a clear understanding of the legal and financial aspects associated with rental property ownership. We'll walk through the stories of successful investors, learning from their triumphs and challenges, and distill their experiences into actionable insights that you can apply to your own endeavors.

As we embark on this exploration of rental property investing, consider this book not just a guide but a companion on your path to financial independence. Whether your goal is to generate passive income, diversify your investment portfolio, or build a legacy for future generations, the principles within these pages will serve as a valuable resource to help you navigate the exciting and rewarding world of rental property investing. Let's embark on this journey together, unlocking the doors to prosperity through the power of real estate.

Overview of Rental Property Investing

Rental property investing is a dynamic and rewarding venture that involves acquiring real estate with the goal of generating income through renting or leasing. This form of investment offers individuals the opportunity to build wealth, create a steady cash flow, and diversify their overall investment portfolio.

At its core, rental property investing revolves around the strategic acquisition and management of residential or commercial properties. Investors aim to capitalize on the growing demand for rental housing or business spaces, leveraging their properties to generate passive income. This income is derived from tenants who pay rent to utilize the space, providing investors with a consistent source of revenue.

The key components of successful rental property investing include thorough market research, financial planning, property selection, effective management, and understanding legal and regulatory considerations. Investors must carefully assess potential properties, considering factors such as location, market trends, and the potential for property appreciation.

Additionally, effective property management is crucial for maintaining the value of the investment and ensuring a positive experience for tenants. This involves tasks such as tenant screening, property maintenance, and addressing legal obligations. Successful investors often employ strategies to maximize rental income, such as setting competitive rent prices and implementing cost-effective maintenance practices.

Rental property investing offers numerous advantages, including the potential for long-term appreciation of property value, tax benefits, and the ability to leverage borrowed capital. However, it also comes with its share of challenges and risks, such as market fluctuations, property management issues, and economic downturns.

Importance of Real Estate in Investment

For a number of strong reasons, real estate is important and will continue to be important in the investing world:

1. **Tangible Asset with Intrinsic Value:** Real estate involves the ownership of tangible assets—land and buildings—which inherently possess intrinsic value. Unlike certain financial instruments, real estate provides a physical and lasting presence, making it a solid and appreciating investment.

2. **Diversification of Investment Portfolio:** Including real estate in an investment portfolio enhances diversification, spreading risk across different asset classes. Real estate often exhibits a low correlation with stocks and bonds, making it a valuable component for risk mitigation and portfolio stability.

3. **Steady Income Stream:** Rental properties offer a consistent and often predictable income stream through rental payments. This steady cash flow can provide investors with a reliable source of passive income, contributing to financial stability and long-term wealth accumulation.

4. **Potential for Appreciation:** Real estate has the potential to appreciate over time, driven by factors such as location, market demand, and property improvements. Appreciation can significantly boost the overall return on investment, making real estate an attractive option for long-term wealth growth.

5. **Leverage and Financing Opportunities:** Real estate investments often allow for leveraging, where investors can use borrowed capital to amplify their purchasing power. This can magnify returns, provided the investment appreciates in value, making real estate an efficient avenue for wealth creation.

6. **Tax Advantages:** Real estate investments come with various tax benefits, including deductions for mortgage interest, property taxes, and certain expenses related to property management. These tax advantages can enhance the overall profitability of real estate investments.

7. **Long-Term Wealth Building:** Real estate's combination of potential appreciation, steady income, and tax advantages positions it as a powerful tool for long-term wealth building. Investors who adopt a strategic and patient approach can witness substantial financial growth over time.

Understanding the importance of real estate in investment involves recognizing its unique qualities and the diverse ways it contributes to a well-balanced and resilient investment portfolio. Whether seeking income, capital appreciation, or risk diversification, real estate remains a cornerstone in the landscape of prudent and strategic investing.

CHAPTER 1:
Understanding Market Dynamics

Understanding market dynamics is essential for businesses seeking sustained success in today's dynamic and competitive business environment. Market dynamics encompass a complex interplay of various forces and factors that shape the behavior and performance of a market. A comprehensive grasp of these dynamics empowers businesses to make informed decisions, adapt to changing conditions, and stay ahead of the competition.

One fundamental aspect of market dynamics is the interaction between supply and demand. The forces of supply and demand dictate pricing and overall market equilibrium. Businesses must constantly monitor and analyze these factors to anticipate fluctuations and set competitive prices that align with consumer expectations.

Competition is another crucial element influencing market dynamics. A competitive analysis helps businesses identify key players, their strategies, strengths, and weaknesses. Recognizing competitive threats and opportunities enables companies to position themselves strategically, differentiate their offerings, and innovate to stay relevant.

Consumer preferences play a pivotal role in shaping market dynamics. Understanding the needs, wants, and behaviors of consumers is essential for product development, marketing strategies, and maintaining customer loyalty. Market research and customer feedback are invaluable tools for gaining insights into changing preferences and adapting strategies accordingly.

Economic conditions, both global and local, significantly impact market dynamics. Factors such as inflation, interest rates, and economic growth influence consumer spending patterns and business investments. Businesses need to be vigilant and responsive to economic shifts to navigate challenges and leverage opportunities that arise.

Technological advancements contribute to market dynamics by shaping how businesses operate and consumers engage with products and services. Embracing innovation and staying abreast of technological trends enable businesses to stay competitive, streamline operations, and meet evolving customer expectations.

Regulatory influences also play a pivotal role in shaping market dynamics. Changes in laws and regulations can impact industries differently, creating opportunities or challenges for businesses. Staying compliant with regulations and anticipating potential changes is crucial for mitigating risks and maintaining a sustainable business model.

Globalization further complicates market dynamics, as businesses must navigate international trade, cultural nuances, and geopolitical factors. An understanding of global markets and geopolitical trends is essential for businesses with international operations or aspirations.

To comprehend market dynamics comprehensively, businesses employ various analytical tools, market research methodologies, and data-driven approaches. Continuous monitoring of industry trends, competitor activities, and consumer feedback provides a real-time understanding of the market landscape.

A nuanced understanding of market dynamics is indispensable for businesses aiming for long-term success. By navigating the intricacies of supply and demand, competition, consumer preferences, economic conditions, technological changes, regulatory influences, and globalization, businesses can adapt, innovate, and thrive in an ever-evolving market.

Market Research and Analysis

Market research and analysis form the bedrock of strategic decision-making for businesses, offering valuable insights into the dynamics of the marketplace. This comprehensive process involves collecting, interpreting, and evaluating data to understand market trends, consumer behavior, and competitive landscapes. Let's delve into the multifaceted aspects of market research and analysis.

1. **Objectives and Scope:**
Market research begins by defining clear objectives. Whether it's launching a new product, entering a new market, or understanding consumer preferences, having well-defined goals shapes the research approach. The scope extends to both quantitative and qualitative data, providing a holistic view of the market.

2. **Types of Market Research:**
There are two main types of market research—primary and secondary. Primary research involves collecting firsthand data, often through surveys, interviews, or focus groups. Secondary research relies on existing data sources, such as industry reports, government publications, or competitor analyses. A combination of both types offers a more robust understanding.

3. **Data Collection Methods:**
In primary research, various data collection methods are employed, including surveys, interviews, observations, and experimental research. These methods allow businesses to gather specific information directly from target audiences, uncovering insights that may not be available through secondary sources alone.

4. **Analyzing Consumer Behavior:**
Understanding consumer behavior is a key focus of market research. Analyzing purchasing patterns, preferences, and decision-making processes provides businesses with actionable intelligence. This insight helps in tailoring products, services, and marketing strategies to meet consumer needs effectively.

5. **Competitor Analysis:**
A vital component of market research is analyzing competitors. This involves studying competitors' products, pricing strategies, market share, and strengths and weaknesses. By benchmarking against industry peers, businesses can identify opportunities for differentiation and strategic positioning.

6. **Market Segmentation:**
Market research enables businesses to divide their target market into segments based on demographics, psychographics, or behavioral characteristics. This segmentation allows for personalized marketing strategies and product development tailored to specific customer segments.

7. **SWOT Analysis:**
Conducting a SWOT analysis (Strengths, Weaknesses, Opportunities, Threats) is a common practice in market research. It helps businesses assess internal strengths and weaknesses while identifying external opportunities and threats, providing a strategic overview for decision-making.

8. **Emerging Trends and Opportunities**:
Market research plays a pivotal role in identifying emerging trends and opportunities. By staying ahead of market shifts, businesses can proactively adjust their strategies, innovate products, and capitalize on untapped markets.

9. **Decision Support:**
Market research serves as a foundation for decision-making. Whether launching a new product, expanding into a new market, or adjusting pricing strategies, data-driven insights minimize risks and increase the likelihood of successful outcomes.

10. **Continuous Monitoring:**
Market research is an ongoing process. Continuous monitoring of market dynamics, consumer trends, and competitive landscapes ensures that businesses stay agile and responsive to changes. Regular updates allow for timely adjustments to strategies in a dynamic business environment.

Market research and analysis are indispensable tools for businesses aiming to navigate the complexities of the marketplace. By adopting a systematic approach to gather, interpret, and apply data, businesses can make informed decisions, mitigate risks, and position themselves strategically for sustained success.

Identifying Profitable Locations

A crucial component of strategic business planning is locating profitable spaces, especially for sectors like retail, hotel, and real estate. The profitability of a business can be greatly impacted by site selection, which affects foot traffic, consumer demographics, and operational efficiency. Let's examine the various factors and approaches that need to be taken into account while choosing lucrative sites.

1. **Demographic Analysis:**

Understanding the demographic profile of a potential location is paramount. Factors such as population size, age distribution, income levels, and lifestyle trends provide insights into the target customer base. Businesses must align their offerings with the preferences and needs of the local population.

2. **Market Research:**

Comprehensive market research involves analyzing local market dynamics, competition, and demand. Assessing the saturation of similar businesses in the area helps identify gaps in the market that a new establishment could fill. This includes studying consumer behavior, purchasing power, and preferences specific to the locality.

3. **Accessibility and Foot Traffic:**

Proximity to transportation hubs, major roads, and public spaces significantly impacts a location's attractiveness. High foot traffic areas increase the visibility of a business and can lead to more potential customers. Analyzing traffic patterns and accessibility ensures the convenience of reaching the establishment.

4. **Competition Analysis:**

Understanding the competitive landscape is crucial. Assessing the presence, strength, and weaknesses of competitors in the chosen location helps businesses identify opportunities for differentiation. It also aids in developing unique value propositions to stand out in the market.

5. **Regulatory Environment:**

Local regulations and zoning laws can have a profound impact on a business's operations. Understanding the regulatory environment of a potential location is essential to ensure compliance and avoid unexpected legal challenges. This includes considerations such as licensing requirements and restrictions.

6. **Economic Indicators:**

Evaluating the economic health of an area is vital. Factors like employment rates, GDP growth, and overall economic stability can indicate the potential for sustained consumer spending. Thriving economies generally offer more opportunities for businesses to thrive.

7. **Cost of Operations:**

Analyzing the cost of operations in a specific location is critical for financial sustainability. This includes factors such as rent, utilities, labor costs, and taxes. Businesses must weigh these operational expenses against the potential revenue to ensure profitability.

8. **Future Development Plans:**

Investigating the local municipality's plans for future development can provide insights into the long-term viability of a location. Upcoming infrastructure projects, urban development, or changes in the neighborhood can impact the business environment positively or negatively.

9. **Technology and Data Analytics:**

Leveraging technology and data analytics tools can enhance location analysis. Geographic information systems (GIS) and other mapping tools help visualize data, providing a deeper understanding of the spatial aspects that influence profitability.

10. **Flexibility and Adaptability:**

Businesses should also consider the adaptability of their operations to changing conditions. A location that may be profitable today could face shifts in demographics or market trends. A flexible business model allows for adjustments to meet evolving demands

Identifying profitable locations is a nuanced process that requires a combination of thorough research, strategic thinking, and adaptability. Businesses that carefully assess demographic, economic, regulatory, and operational factors stand a better chance of selecting locations that align with their objectives and contribute to long-term success.

CHAPTER 2:

Financial Planning for Investments

In order to develop a plan for the best possible investment management, financial planning for investments is a strategic process that includes evaluating risk tolerance, time horizons, and individual or institutional financial goals. A stable financial future, wealth accumulation, and the accomplishment of financial goals all depend on effective financial planning. This is a comprehensive analysis of the main elements of investment financial planning.

1. **Goal Setting:**
The foundation of financial planning for investments lies in defining clear and realistic financial goals. These goals can vary widely, from short-term objectives like buying a home to long-term aspirations such as retirement planning or funding a child's education. Each goal requires a tailored investment strategy.

2. **Risk Assessment:**
Understanding risk tolerance is crucial in crafting an investment plan. Investors need to evaluate their willingness and capacity to withstand fluctuations in the value of their investments. Risk assessment involves considering factors such as age, financial stability, and the ability to recover from potential losses.

3. **Asset Allocation:**
Diversification is a fundamental principle in investment planning. Asset allocation involves spreading investments across different asset classes, such as stocks, bonds, real estate, and cash equivalents. The allocation is based on the investor's risk tolerance, goals, and time horizon.

4. **Investment Vehicles:**
Selecting the right investment vehicles is a critical aspect of financial planning. Depending on the individual's goals and risk profile, investments may include stocks, bonds, mutual funds, exchange-traded funds (ETFs), real estate, or alternative investments. Each vehicle offers unique risk-return profiles.

5. **Tax Planning:**
Optimizing tax efficiency is an integral part of financial planning for investments. Understanding tax implications on various investment gains and income streams helps investors minimize tax liabilities and maximize after-tax returns. Tax-efficient investment strategies can significantly impact overall portfolio performance.

6. **Emergency Fund and Liquidity:**
Financial planning should account for the creation of an emergency fund to cover unforeseen expenses. Maintaining liquidity in the investment portfolio ensures quick access to funds when needed, without relying on the forced sale of long-term assets.

7. **Regular Monitoring and Rebalancing:**
Investment portfolios should be regularly monitored to ensure alignment with financial goals and changing market conditions. Periodic rebalancing—adjusting the asset allocation to restore the desired balance—helps maintain the risk profile and enhances the portfolio's overall efficiency.

8. **Retirement Planning:**
A crucial element of financial planning is preparing for retirement. This involves estimating future income needs, considering sources of retirement income (such as pensions and Social Security), and designing an investment strategy that supports a comfortable retirement lifestyle.

9. **Education Funding:**
For those with education-related financial goals, planning includes estimating future educational expenses, considering inflation, and choosing investment vehicles that align with the time horizon for educational needs.

10. **Professional Advice and Continuous Learning:**
Seeking advice from financial professionals, such as financial planners or investment advisors, can provide valuable insights and expertise. Continuous learning about investment markets, economic trends, and financial planning strategies helps investors make informed decisions.

Financial planning for investments is a dynamic and personalized process that requires careful consideration of individual circumstances and goals. By setting clear objectives, assessing risk tolerance, diversifying investments, optimizing taxes, and staying informed, investors can build a resilient and growth-oriented investment portfolio that aligns with their financial aspirations.

Budgeting and Financial Goals

Budgeting and financial goals are integral components of a sound financial plan, providing a roadmap for individuals and businesses to manage their finances effectively, achieve specific objectives, and secure a stable financial future. Let's explore in detail the key aspects of budgeting and setting financial goals.

Budgeting

1. **Income Assessment:**

Budgeting begins with a comprehensive assessment of income sources. This includes regular earnings, side incomes, and any other sources of cash inflow. Understanding the total income is crucial for creating a realistic budget.

2. **Expense Tracking:**

Analyzing spending patterns is essential. Categorizing and tracking expenses, including fixed and variable costs, helps identify areas where spending can be optimized. This process lays the foundation for creating a balanced budget.

3. **Creating Categories:**

Budgets are typically divided into categories such as housing, utilities, groceries, transportation, entertainment, and savings. Allocating specific amounts to each category ensures that spending aligns with financial priorities.

4. **Emergency Fund Allocation:**

Budgeting includes setting aside funds for an emergency fund. This acts as a financial safety net for unexpected expenses, helping to avoid reliance on credit and maintaining financial stability.

5. **Debt Management:**

Managing existing debts is an integral part of budgeting. Allocating funds for debt repayment helps individuals and businesses reduce interest payments and work towards becoming debt-free.

6. **Savings and Investments:**

Allocating a portion of the budget to savings and investments is crucial for long-term financial stability. This can include contributions to retirement accounts, investment portfolios, and other financial instruments.

7. **Regular Review and Adjustments:**

Budgets should not be static. Regularly reviewing spending patterns, reassessing financial goals, and adjusting the budget as circumstances change ensure its relevance and effectiveness over time.

8. **Financial Literacy:**

Understanding basic financial concepts is essential for effective budgeting. Financial literacy empowers individuals to make informed decisions, manage debt responsibly, and optimize their financial resources.

Financial Goals

1. **Short-Term Goals:**

Short-term financial goals typically have a timeframe of one year or less. These could include building an emergency fund, saving for a vacation, or paying off a credit card.

2. **Medium-Term Goals:**

Medium-term financial goals span one to five years and often involve larger financial commitments. Examples include saving for a down payment on a home, funding education, or starting a business.

3. **Long-Term Goals:**

Long-term financial goals extend beyond five years and often revolve around major life milestones. These can include retirement planning, purchasing a home, or ensuring financial security for future generations.

4. **Specific and Measurable Objectives:**

Financial goals should be specific and measurable. Instead of a vague goal like "saving more money," a specific goal could be "saving $10,000 for a home down payment by the end of the year."

5. **Realistic and Achievable:**

Setting realistic and achievable financial goals is crucial for maintaining motivation. Unrealistic goals can lead to frustration, while achievable goals provide a sense of accomplishment and progress.

6. **Prioritization:**

When multiple financial goals exist, prioritizing them based on urgency and importance is essential. This ensures that resources are allocated efficiently to meet the most critical objectives first.

7. **Flexibility:**

Financial goals should be flexible to adapt to changing circumstances. Life events, economic conditions, and personal priorities may evolve, requiring adjustments to the original goals.

8. **Regular Review and Adjustments:**

Similar to budgeting, financial goals should be regularly reviewed and adjusted as needed. This ensures alignment with changing circumstances and allows for continuous progress towards financial objectives.

Budgeting and financial goals work synergistically to provide individuals and businesses with a structured approach to managing finances. By creating realistic budgets, tracking expenses, and setting specific, measurable, and achievable financial goals, individuals can navigate their financial journey with confidence and work towards achieving long-term financial success.

Financing Options for Rental Properties

Rental property financing options are essential to real estate investing because they provide a variety of ways for investors to purchase and oversee assets that generate income. Comprehending these alternatives is essential for making well-informed choices and maximizing profits. Below is a detailed summary of different financing strategies:

Traditional Mortgages:

- Investors can obtain conventional mortgages with fixed or adjustable interest rates.
- Down payments typically range from 15% to 25%, depending on the lender and loan type.
- These loans are suitable for long-term investments, providing stability with predictable monthly payments.

FHA Loans:

- Federal Housing Administration (FHA) loans are government-backed and often feature lower down payment requirements (as low as 3.5%).
- These loans are accessible to first-time homebuyers, making them appealing for investors entering the real estate market.

VA Loans:

- Veterans Affairs (VA) loans are exclusive to military veterans, offering favorable terms, including zero down payment.
- While primarily intended for owner-occupied homes, some investors leverage VA loans for multifamily properties.
- Commercial Loans:Investors targeting larger rental properties, such as apartment buildings, may opt for commercial loans.
- These loans typically have higher interest rates but offer more flexibility in terms of property type and loan structure.

Private Lenders and Hard Money Loans:

- Private lenders and hard money loans are often sought for shorter-term investments or when traditional financing is challenging.
- Interest rates can be higher, but approval processes are typically faster, making them suitable for quick acquisitions or property improvements.

Seller Financing:

- In this arrangement, the property seller acts as the lender, allowing the buyer to make payments directly to them.
- Terms are negotiable, providing flexibility, but this option depends on the seller's willingness to finance the transaction.

Home Equity Loans and Lines of Credit:

- Seasoned investors might leverage existing property equity through home equity loans or lines of credit to fund new acquisitions.
- This strategy allows for quicker access to capital without involving a traditional mortgage lender.

Real Estate Crowdfunding:
- Crowdfunding platforms pool funds from multiple investors to finance real estate projects.
- Investors can participate with relatively small amounts, gaining access to a diverse range of properties.

Wraparound Mortgages:
- In a wraparound mortgage, an investor assumes an existing mortgage while creating a new one at a higher value.
- This technique can be employed when the existing mortgage terms are favorable, providing an alternative financing structure.

Lease Options:
- Investors can negotiate lease options, allowing them to rent a property with the right to purchase it at a predetermined price.
- This approach provides time for the investor to secure traditional financing while controlling the property.

In conclusion, the world of financing options for rental properties is diverse, catering to investors with varying risk tolerance, financial situations, and investment goals. Successful real estate investors often employ a combination of these strategies, adapting their approach based on market conditions and individual property dynamics. Before selecting a financing option, thorough research and consultation with financial professionals are crucial to ensure alignment with investment objectives and risk management.

CHAPTER 3:

Property Selection and Evaluation

Finding and assessing the ideal property is essential to making profitable real estate investments. The following are crucial factors and actions to take while choosing and assessing properties

1. Define Investment Goals:

- Clearly outline your investment objectives, whether it's long-term rental income, short-term appreciation, or a combination of both. This will guide your property selection criteria.

2. Location Analysis:

- Evaluate the neighborhood's growth potential, amenities, proximity to schools, public transport, and employment centers.
- Consider the area's crime rates and overall safety, as these factors influence both property value and tenant attraction.

3. Market Research:

- Analyze current market trends, property values, and rental rates in the target area.
- Assess the historical performance of the real estate market to make informed predictions about future trends.

4. Property Type:

- Decide on the type of property that aligns with your investment goals, whether it's residential, commercial, or multifamily.
- Consider factors such as property size, layout, and condition.

5. Financial Analysis:

- Conduct a thorough financial analysis, factoring in purchase price, financing costs, property taxes, insurance, and potential maintenance expenses.
- Calculate the potential return on investment (ROI) and cash flow to ensure the property meets your financial expectations.

6. Condition of the Property:

- Inspect the property thoroughly for any structural issues, necessary repairs, or renovations.
- Consider hiring a professional inspector to provide a detailed assessment.

7. Future Development and Zoning:

- Research the local zoning regulations and future development plans in the area to anticipate any changes that may impact property value.

8. Property Management Considerations:

- Evaluate the feasibility of managing the property yourself or hiring a property management company.
- Factor in management costs and how they may affect your overall returns.

9. Tenant Demand:

- Assess the demand for rental properties in the area by understanding vacancy rates and tenant demographics.
- Consider the local job market and population growth, as these factors influence rental demand.

10. Exit Strategy:

- Plan your exit strategy in advance, whether it's selling for appreciation, converting to another use, or passing it down as part of your estate.

11. **Legal and Regulatory Compliance:**
   - Ensure that the property complies with local building codes and regulations.
   - Understand landlord-tenant laws and regulations in the area.

12. **Network and Professional Advice:**
- Build a network of real estate professionals, including agents, attorneys, and inspectors, to provide valuable insights and guidance.
- Seek professional advice, especially if you're new to real estate investment.

13. **Due Diligence:**
   - Verify property records, title, and any liens or encumbrances.
   - Check for any pending legal issues or disputes related to the property.

By diligently considering these factors and conducting thorough research, you increase the likelihood of selecting a property that aligns with your investment goals and proves to be a sound financial decision. Always adapt your approach based on the specific dynamics of each property and the ever-changing real estate market.

Criteria for Choosing Rental Properties

Choosing the right rental property involves careful consideration of various criteria to ensure a successful and profitable investment. Here are key factors to consider:

1. **Location:**
- Proximity to Amenities: Consider the property's accessibility to schools, shopping centers, public transportation, and other essential amenities.
- Neighborhood Quality: Evaluate the safety, cleanliness, and overall appeal of the neighborhood.
- Job Market: Assess the local job market and employment opportunities, as this influences tenant demand.

2. **Property Type and Size:**
- Type of Property: Decide on the type of property (single-family, multi-family, commercial) based on your investment goals and target tenant demographic.
- Size and Layout: Consider the property's size and layout to meet the needs of potential tenants.

3. **Market Conditions:**
   - Supply and Demand: Analyze the current supply and demand for rental properties in the area.
   - Market Trends: Stay informed about market trends, property values, and rental rates to make informed decisions.

4. **Financial Metrics:**
   - Purchase Price: Ensure the property's purchase price aligns with your budget and expected returns.
   - Cash Flow: Evaluate potential cash flow by considering rental income, operating expenses, and financing costs.
   - Return on Investment (ROI): Calculate the expected ROI to gauge the profitability of the investment.

5. **Condition of the Property:**
   - Inspection: Conduct a thorough inspection to identify any necessary repairs or maintenance.
   - Age and Upkeep: Consider the age of the property and the maintenance required to keep it in good condition.

6. **Tenant Demographics:**
- Target Tenant Profile: Define your target tenant profile and choose a property that caters to their needs.
- Local Population Growth: Consider the population growth in the area to assess the potential for a growing tenant pool.

7. **Property Management Considerations:**

- Management Intensity: Evaluate how hands-on the property management will be and assess whether you can handle it yourself or need professional management.
- Management Costs: Factor in the cost of property management if outsourcing the responsibility.

8. **Future Development and Zoning:**
   - Future Plans: Investigate any upcoming developments or changes in the area that may impact property value.
   - Zoning Regulations: Understand local zoning regulations to anticipate potential limitations or opportunities.

9. **Risk Tolerance:**
   - Market Stability: Assess the overall stability of the local real estate market and consider your risk tolerance.
   - Economic Indicators: Keep an eye on economic indicators that may affect property values and rental demand.

10. **Legal and Regulatory Compliance**:
   - Local Regulations: Ensure the property complies with local housing and safety regulations.
   - Landlord-Tenant Laws: Understand the legal framework governing landlord-tenant relationships in the area.

11. **Exit Strategy:**
- Long-Term Plans: Have a clear exit strategy, whether it involves selling, refinancing, or transitioning to a different investment.

12. **Network and Professional Advice:**
- Real Estate Professionals: Build relationships with real estate agents, inspectors, and other professionals for guidance.
- Peer Advice: Seek advice from experienced investors or mentors who have a proven track record.

By carefully considering these criteria, you can make informed decisions that align with your investment objectives and contribute to a successful and sustainable rental property portfolio. Adapt your criteria based on market conditions and your evolving investment strategy over time.

Assessing Property Value and Potential

Assessing property value and potential is a fundamental aspect of real estate investment. A comprehensive evaluation involves considering various factors to determine the current and future worth of a property, as well as its potential for generating returns.

1. **Comparable Sales (Comps):**

Current Market Prices: Analyze recent sales of similar properties in the area to gauge the current market prices
Adjustments: Make adjustments for differences in size, condition, and amenities to accurately compare properties.

2. **Income Approach:Rental Income:**

For income-generating properties, assess potential rental income by considering local rental rates and market demand.
Cap Rate: Calculate the capitalization rate by dividing the property's net operating income (NOI) by its current market value.

3. **Cost Approach:Replacement Cost:**

Estimate the cost of rebuilding the property from scratch, considering current construction costs and depreciation
Land Value: Separate the land value from the overall property value to understand the contribution of the structure.

4. **Location and Neighborhood:Location Factors:**

Evaluate the property's proximity to amenities, schools, employment centers, and transportation hubs.Neighborhood Trends: Consider the overall trends and desirability of the neighborhood, as it significantly impacts property values.

5. **Market Conditions:Market Trends:**

Stay abreast of local market trends, analyzing whether property values are appreciating, stabilizing, or declining.

Economic Indicators: Monitor economic indicators that influence property values, such as employment rates and GDP growth.

6. Physical Condition:Inspection:
Conduct a thorough inspection to assess the property's structural integrity, condition of systems, and potential maintenance or repair needs.
Renovation Costs: Estimate the costs of necessary renovations and improvements that can enhance the property's value.

7. Supply and Demand:Market Dynamics:
Understand the balance between property supply and demand in the local market.
Absorption Rate: Evaluate how quickly properties are selling in the area, indicating market demand.

8. Potential for Appreciation:Development Plans:
Investigate any upcoming developments or infrastructure projects that may positively impact property values.Gentrification: Assess the potential for gentrification in the area, as it can lead to substantial appreciation.

9. Tenant Demand:Historical Vacancy Rates:
Analyze historical vacancy rates in the area to understand tenant demand.
Demographic Trends: Consider demographic factors that may influence the demand for rental properties.

10. Financing and Mortgage Rates:
Interest Rates: Monitor current mortgage rates, as they can affect property values and the affordability of potential buyers.
Financing Availability: Assess the availability of financing options, as it influences the purchasing power of potential buyers.

11. Regulatory and Zoning Factors:
Zoning Changes: Be aware of any potential changes in zoning regulations that may affect property use and value.
Land Use Policies: Understand local land use policies and restrictions that could impact development potential.

12. Comparable Rental Analysis:Rent Comparisons:
Compare rental rates for similar properties in the area to determine competitive market rents.
Vacancy Rates: Assess the historical and current vacancy rates in the rental market.

13. Environmental Factors:Environmental Assessments:
Consider potential environmental issues that could affect property value, such as contamination or flood risks.
Sustainability Trends: Evaluate the impact of sustainability and energy efficiency trends on property values.

14. Exit Strategy Considerations:
Long-Term Viability: Assess whether the property aligns with your long-term investment goals and exit strategy.
Potential for Value-Add: Explore opportunities for value-added improvements that can increase property value.
The assessment of property value and potential is a multifaceted process that requires a holistic understanding of market dynamics, property conditions, and economic factors. Investors must continually adapt their evaluation strategies to reflect changes in the real estate landscape and make informed decisions based on a thorough analysis of these key elements. Successful investors leverage a combination of quantitative data and qualitative insights to maximize returns and mitigate risks in their real estate portfolios.

CHAPTER 4:

Legal and Regulatory Considerations

1. **Fair Housing Laws:** Address the importance of adhering to fair housing laws to avoid discrimination in tenant selection.
2. **Landlord-Tenant Regulations:** Discuss the legal rights and responsibilities of landlords and tenants, including lease agreements, security deposits, and eviction procedures.
3. **Local Zoning Laws:** Emphasize the significance of understanding and complying with local zoning regulations and restrictions.
4. **Property Maintenance Standards:** Highlight the need for landlords to meet minimum property maintenance standards set by local authorities.
5. **Tax Implications:** Provide an overview of tax considerations related to rental income, deductions, and potential benefits for property owners.
6. **Insurance Requirements:** Discuss the types of insurance landlords may need, such as liability insurance and property insurance, to mitigate risks.
7. **Environmental Regulations:** Touch upon environmental regulations that may impact property owners, such as lead paint or asbestos regulations.
8. **Occupancy Limits:** Explain any legal restrictions on the number of occupants in a rental property.
9. Licensing and Permits: Stress the importance of obtaining any required licenses or permits for rental properties.
10. **Tenant Privacy:** Address the legal aspects of tenant privacy rights and the landlord's obligations in handling tenant information.

Always consult with a legal professional to ensure accuracy and compliance with the latest regulations in your specific location.

Landlord-Tenant Laws

Landlord-tenant laws vary by jurisdiction, but here are some common aspects to consider:
1. **Lease Agreements:** Outline the essential elements of a lease agreement, including terms, rent amount, security deposit, and responsibilities of both parties.
2. **Security Deposits:** Explain rules regarding the collection, use, and return of security deposits, including any interest requirements.
3. **Rent Payments:** Clarify the due dates, methods of payment, and any penalties for late payments.
4. **Repairs and Maintenance:** Detail the landlord's responsibilities for maintaining the property and the tenant's obligations for reporting and cooperating with repairs.
5. **Evictions:** Describe the legal process for eviction, the valid reasons for eviction, and any required notices.
6. **Discrimination Laws:** Emphasize compliance with fair housing laws to prevent discrimination based on race, gender, religion, disability, or other protected characteristics.
7. **Entry to the Property:** Address the rules and notice requirements for landlords entering the rental unit, respecting tenant privacy.
8. **Tenant Rights:** Outline the rights of tenants, including the right to a habitable dwelling, privacy, and protection from unlawful eviction.
9. **Lease Termination:** Explain the procedures for ending a lease, including notice periods and potential penalties.
10. **Habitability Standards:** Highlight the legal requirements for maintaining a habitable living environment, including issues related to health and safety.

Remember, specific regulations can vary, so it's crucial to consult local landlord-tenant laws or seek legal advice for accurate and up-to-date information.

Tax Implications for Rental Income

Tax implications for rental income can be complex and are subject to change. It's crucial for property owners to understand these implications to ensure compliance with tax laws.

1. **Rental Income Taxation:**
- Rental income is generally considered taxable. This includes rent received, advance rent, or any services or property provided in exchange for rent.
- Income must be reported on the owner's annual tax return.

2. **Tax Deductible Expenses:**
- Property owners can deduct various expenses related to managing and maintaining the rental property. Common deductions include mortgage interest, property taxes, insurance, utilities, and repairs.
- Depreciation of the property value and certain capital improvements can also be deducted over time.

3. **Depreciation:**
- The IRS allows property owners to depreciate the cost of the building (not the land) over a set period, typically 27.5 years for residential properties.
- Depreciation is a non-cash expense that can reduce taxable income.

4. **Passive Activity Losses:**
- Rental activities are often considered passive income. Losses from passive activities, including rental real estate, may have limitations on deductibility against other types of income.

5. **1031 Exchange:**
- Property owners may use a 1031 exchange to defer capital gains taxes by reinvesting the proceeds from the sale of one property into another of like-kind.

6. **Home Office Deduction:**
- If part of the home is used exclusively for managing rental activities, a home office deduction may be available for associated expenses.

7. **State and Local Taxes:**
- State and local tax laws can vary. Property owners should be aware of specific regulations in their jurisdiction, including any additional taxes on rental income.

8. **Recordkeeping:**
- Keeping thorough and accurate records of income and expenses is crucial for tax purposes. This includes receipts, invoices, and documentation of all financial transactions related to the rental property.

9. **Qualified Business Income Deduction (QBI):**
- The QBI deduction may apply to certain rental income, allowing property owners to deduct up to 20% of qualified income.

10. **Professional Advice:**
- Due to the complexity of tax laws, property owners are strongly advised to seek the guidance of a tax professional or accountant to ensure compliance with current regulations and to optimize tax strategies.

It's important to note that tax laws can change, and the information provided here is a general overview. Property owners should consult with a tax professional for personalized advice based on their specific situation and local regulations.

CHAPTER 5:
Property Management Strategies

1. **Screening Tenants:**
- Implement a thorough tenant screening process to ensure reliable and responsible renters. This may include background checks, credit checks, and rental history verification.

2. **Clear Lease Agreements:**
- Draft comprehensive and legally sound lease agreements. Clearly outline terms, responsibilities, rent due dates, and any specific rules or regulations.

3. **Regular Property Maintenance:**
- Conduct routine inspections and promptly address maintenance issues. Proactive maintenance helps prevent costly repairs and maintains tenant satisfaction.

4. **Responsive Communication:**
- Establish open lines of communication with tenants. Respond promptly to inquiries and concerns to foster positive relationships.

5. **Rent Collection System:**
- Implement a streamlined rent collection process. Consider online payment options to enhance convenience for tenants and reduce late payments.

6. **Emergency Preparedness:**
- Have a plan in place for handling emergencies such as plumbing issues, electrical problems, or natural disasters. Provide tenants with clear emergency procedures.

7. **Legal Compliance:**
- Stay informed about local, state, and federal regulations. Adhere to fair housing laws, building codes, and other legal requirements to avoid legal issues.

8. **Technology Integration:**
- Utilize property management software to streamline tasks like rent collection, maintenance requests, and financial reporting. This can improve efficiency and organization.

9. **Tenant Retention Programs:**
- Implement strategies to retain good tenants. Consider lease renewal incentives, prompt issue resolution, and regular communication to create a positive renting experience.

10. **Budgeting and Financial Planning:**
- Develop a detailed budget that includes operating expenses, maintenance costs, and potential vacancies. Plan for unexpected expenses to maintain financial stability.

11. **Insurance Coverage:**
- Ensure adequate insurance coverage for the property. This may include property insurance, liability coverage, and, in some cases, additional coverage for specific risks.

12. **Community Engagement:**
- Foster a sense of community within the property. Organize events or initiatives that encourage positive interactions among tenants.

13. **Professional Property Management:**
- Consider hiring a professional property management company if managing multiple properties becomes overwhelming. They can handle day-to-day operations, tenant relations, and legal compliance.

14. **Market Analysis:**
- Stay informed about the local real estate market. Regularly assess rental rates and property values to make informed decisions about pricing and investment strategies.

Customize these strategies based on the specific needs of the property and the preferences of both landlords and tenants. Regularly reassess and adjust strategies as market conditions and property dynamics evolve.

Effective Tenant Screening

Effective tenant screening is crucial for finding reliable and responsible tenants who are likely to uphold lease agreements and maintain the property properly.

1. **Rental Application:**
- Require all prospective tenants to complete a detailed rental application. This should include personal information, rental history, employment details, and references.

2. **Credit Check:**
- Obtain the applicant's consent to run a credit check. Review their credit history to assess financial responsibility, outstanding debts, and any previous issues with landlords.

3. **Income Verification:**
- Verify the applicant's income by requesting recent pay stubs, W-2 forms, or tax returns. This ensures they have a stable financial situation to cover rent.

4. **Rental History:**
- Contact previous landlords to inquire about the applicant's rental history. Ask about payment punctuality, adherence to lease terms, and overall conduct as a tenant.

5. **Employment Verification:**
- Verify the applicant's employment status and stability. Contact their employer to confirm income and job security.

6. **Criminal Background Check:**
- Conduct a criminal background check to identify any history of criminal activities. Be aware of local laws regarding the use of criminal records in tenant screening.

7. **Eviction History:**
- Check for any history of evictions. This information can provide insights into a tenant's past rental behavior.

8. **Reference Checks:**
- Contact personal and professional references provided by the applicant. This can provide additional perspectives on the individual's character and reliability.

9. **Rental Criteria:**
- Establish clear rental criteria and apply them consistently to all applicants. This helps avoid discrimination and ensures a fair screening process.

10. **Communication:**
- Communicate openly with applicants about the screening process and criteria. Transparency can help build trust and cooperation.

11. **Legal Compliance:**
- Ensure that your tenant screening process complies with fair housing laws and other relevant regulations. Avoid any discriminatory practices.

12. **Evaluate Red Flags:**
- Look for warning signs, such as gaps in rental history, inconsistent information, or negative feedback from references.

13. **Written Consent:**
- Obtain written consent from applicants before conducting any background checks. This is a legal requirement and emphasizes transparency in the process.

14. **Decision-Making Process:**
- Establish a systematic process for evaluating applicants based on the gathered information. Consider factors such as rental history, credit score, and income stability.

By combining these steps, landlords can make informed decisions about prospective tenants, reducing the risk of issues during the lease term. Always adhere to legal guidelines and treat all applicants fairly and equally.

Maintenance and Repair

In order to protect the value of rental properties and guarantee tenant happiness, upkeep and repairs are crucial. important factors for efficient administration of repairs and maintenance:

1. **Regular Inspections:**

- Conduct regular inspections to identify potential maintenance issues before they escalate. This proactive approach helps address problems early on.

2. Preventive Maintenance:
- Implement a preventive maintenance schedule for systems such as HVAC, plumbing, and electrical. Regular servicing can prevent costly breakdowns.

3. Tenant Communication:
- Encourage tenants to report maintenance issues promptly. Establish clear communication channels to receive and address their concerns in a timely manner.

4. Emergency Response Plan:
- Develop a plan for handling emergency maintenance situations, such as burst pipes or electrical failures. Ensure tenants know the procedures for reporting emergencies.

5. Quality Contractors:
- Build relationships with reliable contractors and service providers. Having a trusted network can lead to quicker response times and quality work.

6. Budgeting for Maintenance:
- Allocate funds in the budget specifically for maintenance and repairs. Planning for these expenses helps prevent financial strain when unexpected issues arise.

7. Documentation:
- Keep thorough records of all maintenance and repair activities. Documenting the work performed, costs, and timelines can be valuable for future reference and financial planning.

8. Tenant Education:
- Educate tenants on basic property maintenance tasks they are responsible for, such as changing air filters or reporting minor issues promptly.

9. Landlord's Responsibilities:
- Clearly communicate what maintenance responsibilities fall under the landlord's purview. This may include structural repairs, major systems, and addressing safety concerns.

10. Timely Repairs:
- Address maintenance requests and repairs promptly. Timely response enhances tenant satisfaction and prevents issues from worsening.

11. Budget for Capital Improvements:
- Plan for larger, periodic improvements such as roof replacements or exterior renovations. Budgeting for these capital improvements helps avoid financial strain in the long term.

12. Compliance with Regulations:
- Ensure that all maintenance activities comply with local building codes and regulations. Failure to adhere to these standards can lead to legal issues.

13. Tenant Communication during Repairs:
- Keep tenants informed during repair processes. Provide realistic timelines and any necessary instructions to minimize disruption to their daily lives.

14. Post-Repair Inspections:
- After repairs are completed, conduct follow-up inspections to ensure the work meets quality standards and the issue has been fully resolved.

15. Continuous Improvement:
- Regularly assess the effectiveness of your maintenance processes and seek ways to improve efficiency, cost-effectiveness, and tenant satisfaction.

By prioritizing maintenance and repair activities, landlords can create a safe and comfortable living environment for tenants while preserving the long-term value of their rental properties.

CHAPTER 6:
Maximizing Rental Income

Key strategies for optimizing your rental property's financial performance:

1. **Market Analysis:**
- Stay informed about local rental market trends. Regularly assess comparable rental rates to set competitive yet profitable prices.

2. **Property Upgrades:**
- Consider cost-effective property upgrades that can increase rental value. This might include modernizing appliances, improving curb appeal, or adding desirable amenities.

3. **Energy-Efficiency Improvements:**
- Implement energy-efficient measures, such as installing energy-efficient appliances or improving insulation. This not only attracts environmentally conscious tenants but also lowers utility costs, potentially allowing for higher rents.

4. **Add Value with Amenities:**
- Evaluate and incorporate desirable amenities that set your property apart, such as in-unit laundry, high-speed internet, or outdoor spaces. Tenants may be willing to pay more for added conveniences.

5. **Flexible Lease Terms:**
- Offer flexible lease terms to accommodate diverse tenant needs. This could include shorter lease options or the option to renew at a fixed rate.

6. **Regular Rent Reviews:**
- Periodically review rental rates and adjust them based on market conditions and property improvements. Incremental increases can add up over time.

7. **Professional Property Management:**
- Consider hiring a professional property management company to optimize rental income. They can handle marketing, tenant relations, and property maintenance, maximizing efficiency.

8. **Tenant Retention:**
- Focus on tenant satisfaction to encourage lease renewals. Happy, long-term tenants provide a stable income stream and reduce turnover-related costs.

9. **Renters Insurance Requirement:**
- Mandate renters insurance, which not only protects tenants but also safeguards your property. This can provide an added layer of financial security.

10. **Invest in High-Demand Locations:**
- When acquiring new properties, target high-demand areas with strong rental markets. Location significantly influences rental income potential.

11. **Rent Differentiation:**
- Consider tiered rental rates based on factors like property size, location within the building, or the inclusion of specific amenities. This allows you to cater to different tenant preferences.

12. **Automated Rent Payments:**
- Implement automated rent collection methods to ensure timely payments. This reduces late payments and improves overall cash flow.

13. **Regular Property Assessments:**
- Periodically reassess your property's value and potential for rental income. This can involve evaluating market trends, making necessary updates, and adjusting strategies accordingly.

14. **Diversify Rental Streams:**
- Explore additional revenue streams, such as offering storage space, parking, or other services that align with tenant needs and local demand.

15. **Tax Deductions:**
- Take advantage of applicable tax deductions related to your rental property. Consult with a tax professional to ensure you're maximizing tax benefits.

Remember to strike a balance between maximizing income and providing value to tenants to maintain a sustainable, profitable rental property. Regularly reassess and adjust strategies based on market conditions and the evolving needs of your target tenants.

Setting Rent Prices

1. **Market Research:**
- Conduct thorough market research to understand current rental trends in your area. Analyze similar properties to gauge their rental prices.

2. **Comparable Properties:**
- Compare your property to similar ones in terms of size, location, amenities, and overall condition. This helps establish a competitive yet realistic rent.

3. **Local Market Conditions:**
- Consider local market conditions, such as demand, vacancy rates, and economic trends. A high-demand area may support higher rents.

4. **Property Features and Amenities:**
- Assess the unique features and amenities your property offers. Properties with added conveniences may command higher rents.

5. **Operating Costs:**
- Factor in your operating costs, including property taxes, insurance, maintenance, and any utilities covered by the landlord. Ensure that rent covers these expenses and provides a profit.

6. **Tenant Affordability:**
- Consider the target demographic for your property and their likely income levels. Set rents at a level that is affordable for your target tenants.

7. **Comparable Rent Analysis Tools:**
- Utilize online tools or services that provide insights into comparable rents in your area. These tools can offer data-driven perspectives on market rates.

8. **Local Rent Control Laws:**
- Be aware of any local rent control laws or regulations that may impact your ability to set rental prices. Ensure compliance with any rent control restrictions.

9. **Seasonal Variations:**
- Consider seasonal variations that may affect rental demand in your area. Adjust rents accordingly to account for peak or off-peak periods.

10. **Negotiation Flexibility:**
- Assess whether you have flexibility for negotiation. Offering slight flexibility in rent can attract quality tenants and lead to longer-term leases.

11. **Future Rent Increases:**
- Include provisions in your lease agreement for future rent increases, outlining when and how they will occur. This provides clarity for tenants and helps with financial planning.

12. **Tenant Retention:**
- While setting rents, factor in the importance of tenant retention. It may be more cost-effective to maintain existing tenants rather than constantly seeking new ones.

13. **Online Listing Platforms:**
- Use online listing platforms to research comparable properties and understand their rental pricing strategies. This can provide valuable insights into market dynamics.

14. **Professional Advice:**
- Consult with real estate professionals, property managers, or appraisers for expert advice on setting optimal rent prices. Their experience and knowledge of the local market can be invaluable.

15. **Regular Rent Reviews:**
- Periodically review and adjust rent prices based on changes in the local market, property improvements, or economic conditions.

Remember to strike a balance between maximizing rental income and setting reasonable rents to attract and retain quality tenants. Regularly reassess rent pricing strategies to remain competitive in the market.

Strategies for Increasing Cash Flow

A mix of optimizing rental income, cutting costs, and making wise financial decisions are needed to increase cash flow in real estate. The following are methods to increase cash flow:

1. **Rental Rate Optimization:**
- Regularly review local market conditions and adjust rental rates based on demand and comparable property prices to maximize income.

2. **Tenant Retention:**
 - Focus on keeping existing tenants satisfied to reduce turnover costs. Consider offering lease renewal incentives or maintaining open communication.

3. **Property Upgrades:**
- Invest in cost-effective property improvements that can justify higher rental rates. Modern amenities or energy-efficient upgrades can add value.

4. **Energy Efficiency:**
- Implement energy-efficient measures to reduce utility costs. This not only attracts environmentally conscious tenants but also contributes to long-term cost savings.

5. **Additional Revenue Streams:**
- Explore additional income sources, such as offering storage space, parking, or charging fees for specific services that cater to tenant needs and local demand.

6. **Cutting Unnecessary Expenses:**
- Regularly review operating expenses and identify areas for cost-cutting. Negotiate with vendors, look for more cost-effective service providers, and eliminate unnecessary expenditures.

7. **Professional Property Management:**
- Consider hiring a professional property management company to handle day-to-day operations efficiently, ensuring optimal cash flow and freeing up your time.

8. **Rent Payment Automation:**
- Implement automated rent collection methods to reduce late payments and streamline cash flow. This can improve consistency and predictability.

9. **Lease Length Considerations:**
- Offer longer lease terms to secure stable rental income over an extended period. This can reduce turnover and vacancy-related costs.

10. **Tax Planning:**
- Strategically plan for tax deductions and benefits related to your property. Consult with a tax professional to optimize your tax strategy and potentially increase cash flow.

11. **Refinancing:**
- Explore opportunities for refinancing your mortgage if interest rates have decreased. This can result in lower monthly mortgage payments and increased cash flow.

12. **Negotiate with Service Providers:**
- Negotiate with utility providers, maintenance services, and other vendors to secure favorable rates. Lowering operational costs directly impacts cash flow.

Implementing a combination of these strategies tailored to your specific property and market conditions can help maximize cash flow and enhance the financial viability of your real estate investments. Regularly reassess and adjust your approach based on evolving market dynamics and property performance.

CHAPTER 7:

Risk Management

An essential component of real estate investing is risk management, which entails techniques for locating, evaluating, and reducing any risks. For real estate risk management to be effective, keep the following points in mind:

1. **Risk Identification:**
- Thoroughly identify and categorize potential risks associated with your real estate investment. This includes market fluctuations, property-specific issues, and external economic factors.

2. **Market Analysis:**
- Conduct a comprehensive analysis of the local real estate market. Understand trends, demand patterns, and potential economic influences to anticipate market-related risks.

3. **Due Diligence:**
- Perform thorough due diligence before acquiring a property. This includes property inspections, title searches, and reviewing historical financial performance to uncover any hidden risks.

4. **Financial Risk Assessment:**
- Assess financial risks related to mortgage rates, interest rate fluctuations, and overall economic conditions. Evaluate how these factors could impact property cash flow and values.

5. Property Inspection and Maintenance:
- Regular property inspections and proactive maintenance help identify and address potential issues before they escalate, reducing the risk of significant repair costs.

6. **Insurance Coverage:**
- Adequate insurance coverage is essential. Review and update your insurance policies regularly to ensure they provide comprehensive protection against various risks, including natural disasters and liability issues.

7. **Legal and Regulatory Compliance:**
- Stay informed about local zoning laws, building codes, and other regulations. Non-compliance can lead to legal issues, fines, and disruptions to your investment.

8. **Diversification:**
- Diversify your real estate portfolio to spread risk across different property types and locations. This helps mitigate the impact of market-specific or property-specific issues.

9. **Emergency Preparedness:**
- Develop and implement emergency preparedness plans for natural disasters, property damage, or other unforeseen events. Being prepared can minimize the impact of emergencies.

10. **Market Risk Mitigation:**
- Employ strategies to mitigate market risks, such as interest rate risk. This may include fixed-rate mortgages, interest rate hedging, or refinancing at opportune times.

11. **Tenant Selection and Retention:**
- Implement rigorous tenant screening processes to reduce the risk of rent defaults or property damage. Prioritize tenant retention to minimize turnover-related costs.

12. **Financial Reserves:**
- Maintain financial reserves to cover unexpected expenses, periods of vacancy, or economic downturns. Having a financial buffer enhances your ability to weather unforeseen challenges.

13. **Regular Financial Analysis:**
- Conduct regular financial analyses of your properties. Monitor income, expenses, and overall cash flow to identify potential issues and address them proactively.

14. **Professional Guidance:**
- Seek advice from real estate professionals, financial advisors, and legal experts. Their expertise can help you navigate complex risks and make informed decisions.

15. **Continuous Monitoring and Adaptation:**
- Regularly monitor the real estate market, economic conditions, and the performance of your properties. Be ready to adapt your strategies based on changing circumstances.

By adopting a comprehensive risk management approach, real estate investors can navigate uncertainties and enhance the resilience of their investment portfolios. Regular monitoring, adaptation, and proactive measures contribute to long-term success in the real estate market.

Insurance and Liability

Insurance and liability management are crucial aspects of real estate investment to protect assets, mitigate risks, and ensure financial security.

1. **Property Insurance:**
- Obtain comprehensive property insurance to protect against risks such as fire, vandalism, natural disasters, and theft. This coverage helps repair or replace the property in case of damage.

2. **Liability Insurance:**
- Carry liability insurance to protect against claims for bodily injury or property damage that may occur on your property. This coverage is essential for safeguarding against legal liabilities.

3. **Umbrella Insurance:**
- Consider umbrella insurance, which provides additional liability coverage beyond the limits of standard policies. This extra layer of protection can be valuable in case of major lawsuits.

4. **Landlord Insurance:**
- If you're renting out properties, invest in landlord insurance. This specialized coverage typically includes property protection as well as liability coverage for landlord-related risks.

5. **Title Insurance:**
- When acquiring a property, secure title insurance to protect against potential defects or issues with the property title. This coverage helps avoid legal challenges to ownership.

6. **Flood Insurance:**
- Depending on the property's location, consider obtaining flood insurance to protect against flood-related damages. Standard property insurance often excludes coverage for floods.

7. **Business Interruption Insurance:**
- Explore business interruption insurance, which provides coverage for lost rental income in case the property becomes uninhabitable due to covered damages.

8. **Workers' Compensation:**
- If you have on-site employees, ensure compliance with workers' compensation requirements. This coverage protects employees in case of work-related injuries or illnesses.

9. **Review Policy Limits:**
- Regularly review the coverage limits of your insurance policies to ensure they adequately reflect the current value of your property and potential liabilities.

10. **Risk Assessment:**
- Conduct a thorough risk assessment to identify potential liabilities associated with your property. Tailor insurance coverage to address specific risks relevant to your investment.

11. **Legal Compliance:**
- Ensure that your insurance policies comply with local regulations and legal requirements. Failure to comply could lead to gaps in coverage and potential legal issues.

12. **Tenant Insurance Requirements:**
- Mandate tenants to carry renters' insurance. This not only protects their personal belongings but also minimizes potential liability for the property owner in case of tenant-related incidents.

13. **Document Maintenance:**
- Keep detailed records of property maintenance and repairs. Proper documentation can be crucial in the event of insurance claims or legal disputes.

14. **Regular Policy Reviews:**
- Periodically review your insurance policies to ensure they remain current and aligned with your investment strategy. Update coverage as needed, especially when acquiring new properties.

15. **Legal Consultation:**

- Consult with legal professionals to ensure your insurance coverage aligns with local laws and regulations. Legal advice can help you navigate complex liability issues effectively.

By carefully managing insurance coverage and addressing potential liabilities, real estate investors can protect their assets and minimize financial risks associated with property ownership. Regular reviews and adjustments to insurance policies contribute to a comprehensive risk management strategy.

Mitigating Risks in Real Estate Investments

Mitigating risks in real estate investments is crucial for safeguarding assets and ensuring long-term financial success.

1. **Diversification:**
 - Diversify your real estate portfolio by investing in different types of properties and locations. This helps spread risk and reduces the impact of market-specific issues.

2. **Thorough Due Diligence:**
- Conduct comprehensive due diligence before acquiring a property. This includes property inspections, title searches, and a thorough understanding of the local market conditions.

3. **Market Research:**
- Stay informed about local market trends and economic conditions. Regularly analyze supply and demand dynamics, rental rates, and potential economic influences.

4. **Risk Identification:**
- Systematically identify and categorize potential risks associated with your investment. This includes market risks, property-specific risks, and external economic factors.

5. **Insurance Coverage:**
- Obtain comprehensive insurance coverage, including property insurance, liability insurance, and potentially umbrella insurance. Regularly review and update your policies to ensure adequate protection.

6. **Legal Compliance:**
- Ensure compliance with local laws, zoning regulations, and building codes. Non-compliance can lead to legal issues and additional risks.

7. **Financial Reserves:**
- Maintain financial reserves to cover unexpected expenses, periods of vacancy, or economic downturns. Having a financial buffer enhances your ability to weather unforeseen challenges.

8. **Tenant Screening:**
- Implement rigorous tenant screening processes to minimize the risk of rent defaults, property damage, or other tenant-related issues.

9. **Regular Property Inspections:**
- Conduct regular property inspections to identify potential maintenance issues early on. Proactive maintenance helps prevent larger, more costly problems.

10. **Emergency Preparedness:**
- Develop and implement emergency preparedness plans for natural disasters, property damage, or other unforeseen events. Being prepared can minimize the impact of emergencies.

11. **Investment Goals Alignment:**
- Ensure that your investment strategy aligns with your financial goals and risk tolerance. Understanding your objectives helps guide decision-making.

12. **Professional Advice:**
- Seek advice from real estate professionals, financial advisors, and legal experts. Their expertise can provide valuable insights and help you navigate complex risks effectively.

13. **Tenant Retention:**
- Prioritize tenant satisfaction to encourage lease renewals and reduce turnover-related risks. Happy, long-term tenants contribute to a stable income stream.

14. **Market Risk Mitigation:**

- Employ strategies to mitigate market risks, such as interest rate risk. This may include fixed-rate mortgages, interest rate hedging, or refinancing at opportune times.

15. **Continuous Monitoring:**

- Regularly monitor the real estate market, economic conditions, and the performance of your properties. Be ready to adapt your strategies based on changing circumstances.

By combining these strategies and staying vigilant, real estate investors can proactively manage risks and increase the likelihood of long-term success in their investment endeavors. Regular reassessment and adaptation to changing market conditions are integral components of effective risk mitigation in real estate.

CHAPTER 8:

Exit Strategies

For investors in rental properties, exit strategies are essential because they provide flexibility and risk control. Refinancing to gain access to equity, selling the property for a profit, or transferring to long-term ownership for steady rental income are examples of common exit plans. Choosing the best exit strategy requires an understanding of financial objectives, property appreciation potential, and market trends. An investor's capacity to adjust to shifting market conditions and maximize profits can be further improved by diversifying their investments across a range of properties or geographical areas. A dynamic and resilient approach to rental property investing is ensured by periodically reevaluating the portfolio and modifying exit options in response to market conditions.

1. **Sell for Profit:**
- Timing is Key: Consider selling when the property has appreciated significantly, aligning with market trends for optimal returns.
- Market Analysis: Regularly monitor local real estate trends to identify peak selling opportunities.

2. **Refinance for Equity Access:**
- Interest Rate Environment: Assess the current interest rate landscape for favorable refinancing terms, allowing access to additional funds.
- Property Appreciation: Higher property values can facilitate a more substantial cash-out refinance, providing liquidity.

3. **Long-Term Ownership:**
- Stable Income Stream: Hold onto properties for steady rental income, especially in areas with consistent demand and low vacancy rates.
- Tax Benefits: Long-term ownership can offer tax advantages, including depreciation deductions and potential capital gains tax benefits.

4. **Diversification Strategies:**
- Geographic Diversity: Spread investments across different locations to mitigate risks associated with localized market fluctuations.
- Property Types: Owning a mix of property types (residential, commercial) can provide a balanced and resilient portfolio.

5. **Adaptation to Market Conditions:**
- Flexibility: Stay attuned to economic indicators and adjust exit strategies accordingly to align with prevailing market conditions.
- Risk Mitigation: Diversify investments to minimize exposure to specific economic or regional risks.

6. **Regular Portfolio Reassessment:**
- Performance Evaluation: Periodically assess the performance of each property in the portfolio, considering factors like rental income, expenses, and market trends.
- Strategic Adjustments: Modify exit strategies based on changes in personal financial goals, market dynamics, or shifts in the overall investment landscape.

7. **Consideration of Financing Options:**
- Loan Terms: Evaluate the terms of existing loans and explore refinancing options to optimize cash flow or extract equity.
- Risk Management: Assess the impact of interest rate changes on mortgage payments and consider locking in favorable rates.

Ultimately, successful rental property investing involves a dynamic and strategic approach, blending short-term gains with long-term stability while adapting to evolving market conditions. Regularly reassessing and refining exit strategies ensures investors are well-positioned to maximize returns and navigate the complexities of real estate investing.

Selling Rental Properties

When selling rental properties, it's essential to navigate the process strategically for optimal returns and a smooth transaction. Consider the following steps:

1. **Market Analysis:**
   - Evaluate current real estate market conditions in the property's location.
   - Understand local property values and demand to set a competitive listing price.

2. **Financial Review:**
   - Assess the property's financial performance, including rental income, expenses, and potential future costs.
   - Gather all relevant financial documentation for potential buyers.

3. **Tenant Communication:**
   - If tenants occupy the property, communicate transparently about the sale.
   - Consider offering incentives for cooperation, such as flexibility in lease terms or assistance with relocation.

4. **Prepare the Property:**
   - Enhance curb appeal and address any necessary repairs or improvements.
   - Stage the property to showcase its potential, both for investors and owner-occupiers.

5. **Legal and Regulatory Compliance:**
   - Ensure compliance with local laws and regulations related to rental property sales.
   - Provide required documentation, such as tenant leases and property disclosures.

6. **Marketing Strategy:**
   - Develop a comprehensive marketing plan to reach potential buyers.
   - Utilize online platforms, real estate listings, and targeted advertising to maximize exposure.

7. **Negotiation and Offers:**
   - Evaluate offers carefully, considering not only the purchase price but also the terms and conditions.
   - Be prepared to negotiate and seek the best deal that aligns with your financial goals.

8. **Due Diligence:**
- Facilitate due diligence for potential buyers, providing access to necessary documentation and property information.
- Address any concerns or questions promptly to maintain the transaction's momentum.

9. **Closing Process:**
   - Work closely with the buyer, real estate agents, and legal professionals to facilitate a smooth closing process.
   - Ensure all required paperwork is completed accurately and in a timely manner.

10. **Tax Implications:**
    - Understand the tax implications of the sale, including potential capital gains taxes.
    - Consult with a tax professional to optimize your tax strategy.

11. **Reinvestment Strategy:**
- Plan for the proceeds from the sale, considering potential reinvestment in other real estate opportunities or alternative investments.

Remember, each property sale is unique, and adapting to specific circumstances is crucial. Engaging with real estate professionals, including agents and legal advisors, can provide valuable guidance throughout the selling process.

1031 Exchange and Tax Planning

A 1031 Exchange, so called because it is modeled after Internal Revenue Code Section 1031, offers real estate investors a useful tax planning tool to postpone paying capital gains taxes when they sell one property and buy another. The following are important details about tax planning and 1031 exchanges:

1. **Qualifying Properties:**
- The exchange applies to "like-kind" properties, which broadly means real estate used for investment or business purposes.
- Both the relinquished property (property being sold) and the replacement property must meet certain criteria.

2. **Timing Considerations:**
- Strict timelines apply: identify potential replacement properties within 45 days of selling the relinquished property and complete the exchange within 180 days.
- These deadlines are non-negotiable, emphasizing the importance of careful planning and execution.

3. **Qualified Intermediary (QI):**
- A QI is an essential third party involved in the exchange process.
- The QI holds the proceeds from the sale of the relinquished property and uses them to acquire the replacement property, ensuring the investor doesn't take possession of the funds.

4. **Tax Deferral Benefits:**
- Capital gains taxes on the sale of the relinquished property are deferred until the replacement property is eventually sold without a 1031 Exchange.
- This allows investors to preserve more of their capital for reinvestment and property acquisition.

5. **Property Identification Rules:**
- Investors can identify up to three replacement properties without regard to their fair market value or any number of properties as long as their combined value doesn't exceed 200% of the relinquished property's value.
- Identifying replacement properties accurately is crucial to a successful exchange.

6. **Boot" Considerations:**
- Receiving any form of cash, personal property, or mortgage relief (reduction in liabilities) in the exchange is termed "boot."
- Boot received may be subject to immediate taxation, reducing the tax benefits of the 1031 Exchange.

7. **Use with Tax Planning Strategies:**
- Investors often incorporate 1031 Exchanges into broader tax planning strategies.
- This may include coordinating exchanges with estate planning, depreciation recapture planning, or transitioning from active to passive investment strategies.

8. **Replacement Property Selection:**
- Investors should carefully evaluate potential replacement properties based on investment goals, market conditions, and long-term strategy.
- Consider factors such as cash flow potential, location, and future appreciation.

9. **Professional Guidance:**
- Due to the complexity of 1031 Exchanges, investors should seek advice from tax professionals, real estate attorneys, and Qualified Intermediaries to ensure compliance with IRS regulations and maximize tax benefits.

By understanding and effectively utilizing 1031 Exchanges, investors can defer capital gains taxes, optimize their real estate portfolios, and strategically plan for long-term wealth accumulation. Professional guidance is essential to navigate the intricacies of this tax planning strategy successfully.

CHAPTER 9:

Real-life Case Studies

Case Study 1: Successful 1031 Exchange

Investor Profile:

- Objective: Tax deferral and portfolio optimization.
- Property A: Duplex in a rapidly appreciating urban area.
- Property B: Identical duplex in a nearby neighborhood.

Strategy:

1. The investor, recognizing the potential capital gains tax on Property A, decides to leverage a 1031 Exchange.
2. Property A is sold for a substantial profit, and the investor identifies Property B as the replacement within the 45-day window.
3. The 1031 Exchange is executed successfully, with the investor using the proceeds from Property A to acquire Property B.
4. The new property is in an area poised for continued growth, providing both rental income and potential appreciation.

Outcome:

- Capital gains taxes on the sale of Property A are deferred.
- The investor not only preserves their capital for reinvestment but also strategically positions themselves in a high-appreciation market, enhancing long-term portfolio value.

Case Study 2: Strategic Portfolio Diversification

Investor Profile:

- Objective: Diversification and risk mitigation.
- Portfolio: Mix of residential and commercial properties in a single metropolitan area.
- Market Condition: Economic uncertainty and potential market fluctuations.

Strategy:

1. The investor conducts a comprehensive review of their portfolio, recognizing the concentration of assets in a specific location and property type.
2. Decision to sell a portion of residential properties and reinvest in a mix of commercial properties in different geographical locations.
3. Proceeds from property sales are strategically reinvested based on market analyses and future growth projections.

Outcome:

- Diversification reduces exposure to local market risks and provides a more balanced portfolio.
- Commercial properties offer stable income streams and potential for increased value, contributing to a resilient and adaptable investment strategy.

These case studies highlight the importance of strategic decision-making in real estate investing, whether through tax-deferred exchanges or portfolio diversification. Every investor's situation is unique, requiring careful analysis of market conditions, financial goals, and a proactive approach to navigate the dynamic real estate landscape successfully.

Successful Rental Property Investment Stories

Story 1: "Strategic Renovation Yields High Returns"

Investor Profile:

- Objective: Increase property value through strategic renovations for higher rental income and appreciation.

Key Steps:

1. Property Selection: The investor identifies an undervalued property in an up-and-coming neighborhood with potential for growth.

2. Thorough Analysis: Before purchase, the investor conducts a comprehensive analysis of the local market, identifying renovation opportunities that align with tenant preferences.

3. Strategic Renovations: The investor carefully renovates the property, focusing on key improvements that significantly enhance its appeal, such as modernizing the kitchen, upgrading flooring, and improving curb appeal.

4. Rent Adjustment: After renovations are complete, the investor strategically adjusts rental rates to reflect the property's enhanced features and the increased demand in the area.

Outcome:

- The property attracts quality tenants willing to pay premium rents.
- The strategic renovations substantially increase the property's value, allowing the investor to capitalize on both rental income and potential appreciation.

Story 2: "Diversification Across Markets for Stable Income"

Investor Profile:

- Objective: Build a diversified rental portfolio for stable, long-term income.

Key Steps:

1. Market Research: The investor conducts extensive market research to identify multiple promising rental markets across different regions.

2. Property Acquisition: Properties are strategically acquired in various locations, encompassing both residential and commercial real estate.

3. Risk Mitigation: The investor prioritizes diversification to mitigate risks associated with localized economic downturns or shifts in market dynamics.

4. Professional Management: Engages professional property management services to efficiently oversee the diverse portfolio.

Outcome:

- The diversified portfolio provides consistent rental income, even if one market experiences challenges.
- Property values and rental demand across different regions contribute to overall portfolio stability, demonstrating the effectiveness of a well-balanced investment strategy.

These success stories underscore the importance of strategic planning, market research, and proactive decision-making in rental property investment. Whether through targeted renovations or geographic diversification, successful investors navigate challenges by adapting to market conditions and maximizing the potential of their real estate assets.

Learning from Challenges and Failures

Scenario 1: "Market Downturn and Overleveraging"

Challenge:

- Situation: An investor heavily leverages multiple properties in a market that experiences an unexpected downturn.
- Outcome: Rental incomes decrease, property values drop, and the investor faces financial strain due to high mortgage payments.

Key Lessons:

1. Risk Management: Overleveraging amplifies risk during market fluctuations. Lesson learned is to maintain a conservative approach to financing.
2. Market Research: A more thorough analysis of market trends and economic indicators could have provided early warnings and informed a more strategic investment approach.
3. Emergency Fund: Establishing an emergency fund for unforeseen circumstances is crucial to weather financial challenges during market downturns.

Scenario 2: "Tenant Management and Legal Pitfalls"

Challenge:

- Situation:*An investor encounters difficulties in tenant management, including legal disputes and property damage issues.
- Outcome: Legal battles result in financial losses, property damages are not promptly addressed, and the overall reputation of the investor suffers.

Key Lessons:

1. Thorough Tenant Screening: Screening tenants rigorously to ensure they align with lease terms and are likely to be responsible renters can prevent future complications.
2. Legal Understanding: Investors need a solid understanding of landlord-tenant laws and local regulations to navigate disputes effectively and avoid legal pitfalls.
3. Property Management: Outsourcing property management or developing robust in-house management practices can alleviate the burden of day-to-day tenant issues.

Common Lessons:

1. Continuous Education: Regularly staying updated on market trends, legal changes, and industry best practices is essential for long-term success.
2. Diversification: Diversifying investments across different markets and property types can help mitigate risks associated with localized challenges.
3. Adaptability: The ability to adapt to changing market conditions, tenant dynamics, and unforeseen challenges is crucial for sustained success in real estate investment.

Learning from challenges and failures is an inherent part of the investment journey. These experiences provide valuable insights, allowing investors to refine their strategies, improve risk management practices, and ultimately become more resilient in the ever-evolving landscape of real estate.

CHAPTER 10 :
Future Trends in Rental Property Investing

Predicting future trends in rental property investing involves considering various factors, including economic shifts, societal changes, and technological advancements.

1. **Technology Integration:**
- Smart Home Features: Increasing demand for rental properties equipped with smart home technologies, such as automated security systems, thermostats, and energy-efficient appliances.
- Virtual Property Tours: Continued use of virtual reality and augmented reality for remote property tours, making it more convenient for tenants and investors alike.

2. **Sustainable and Green Investments:**
- Growing interest in environmentally sustainable and energy-efficient properties, aligning with the global push for greener living.
- Implementation of eco-friendly features, such as solar panels, energy-efficient windows, and sustainable construction materials.

3. **Flexibility in Rental Models:**
- Co-Living Spaces: Rising popularity of co-living arrangements and shared housing models, catering to the preferences of younger generations.
- Short-Term Rentals: A potential increase in short-term rental investments, driven by the popularity of platforms like Airbnb and a shift in tenant preferences.

4. **Focus on Suburban and Secondary Markets:**
- Increased interest in suburban and secondary markets as remote work becomes more prevalent, with tenants seeking affordability and a change in lifestyle.
- Potential for increased property values and demand in suburban areas with good connectivity to urban centers.

5. **Affordable Housing Initiatives:**
- A growing emphasis on affordable housing solutions, driven by social and economic factors, with investors exploring opportunities to contribute to community development.
- Collaboration between investors and government initiatives to address housing affordability challenges.

6. **Data Analytics for Decision-Making:**
- Greater reliance on data analytics tools to inform investment decisions, property management strategies, and market predictions.
- Use of predictive analytics to identify potential growth areas and assess the risk-return profile of specific investments.

7. **Innovative Financing Models:**
- Development of alternative financing models, including crowdfunding and real estate investment trusts (REITs), providing investors with more diverse investment options.
- Increased adoption of blockchain technology for property transactions, enhancing transparency and efficiency.

8. **Focus on Tenant Experience:**
- A shift towards prioritizing tenant experience, with landlords offering enhanced amenities, community-focused spaces, and improved property management services.
- Tenant satisfaction becomes a crucial factor in property value and long-term investment success.

It's essential for investors to stay abreast of these trends, adapting their strategies to align with evolving market dynamics. Continuous learning, flexibility, and a forward-looking approach are key to navigating the changing landscape of rental property investing successfully.

Technological Innovations

Technological innovations in rental property investing are transforming the way investors manage properties, engage with tenants, and make data-driven decisions. Here are some notable technological trends in the industry:

1. **Smart Home Automation:**
- Integration of smart devices, including thermostats, locks, security systems, and lighting, to enhance security, energy efficiency, and overall tenant experience.

- Remote management capabilities for property owners and managers.

2. Blockchain in Real Estate Transactions:
- Utilization of blockchain technology for secure and transparent real estate transactions, reducing fraud and streamlining the property transfer process.
- Potential for tokenization of real estate assets, allowing for fractional ownership.

3. Artificial Intelligence (AI) in Property Management:
- AI-powered property management platforms that automate routine tasks, such as rent collection, maintenance requests, and communication with tenants.
- Predictive analytics for market trends and property performance.

4. Virtual and Augmented Reality (VR/AR):
- Virtual property tours and augmented reality applications for visualizing property modifications or renovations before implementation.
- VR/AR tools for remote property inspections and virtual staging.

5. Online Platforms for Tenant Screening and Leasing:
- Online platforms that use data analytics for efficient tenant screening, helping landlords make informed leasing decisions.
- E-signature solutions for digital lease agreements and streamlined documentation processes.

6. PropTech Startups:
- Growth of PropTech startups offering innovative solutions for various aspects of real estate, including property management, investment analysis, and tenant engagement.
- Platforms facilitating real-time communication between landlords and tenants.

7. Predictive Analytics for Investment Decisions:
- Advanced data analytics tools for predicting property market trends, identifying potential investment opportunities, and assessing risk.
- Real-time market data and performance metrics to guide investment strategies.

8. Energy Management Solutions:
- Adoption of energy management technologies, such as smart meters and sensors, to monitor and optimize energy usage in rental properties.
- Implementation of energy-efficient systems for cost savings and environmental sustainability.

9. Robotic Process Automation (RPA):
- Use of RPA to automate repetitive tasks in property management, such as data entry, invoicing, and maintenance scheduling.
- Improved operational efficiency and reduced manual workload for property managers.

10. Cybersecurity Measures:
- Increased focus on cybersecurity to protect sensitive tenant data and financial transactions.
- Implementation of secure communication channels and encryption protocols in property management platforms.

Embracing these technological innovations allows rental property investors to enhance operational efficiency, improve tenant satisfaction, and make more informed decisions in a rapidly evolving real estate landscape. Continuous monitoring of emerging technologies can provide investors with a competitive edge in the market.

Evolving Market Trends

Several evolving market trends are shaping the landscape of real estate investing.

1. **Remote Work Impact:**
   - Increased demand for properties in suburban or rural areas as remote work becomes more prevalent.
   - A shift in priorities towards home offices and spaces conducive to remote work.

2. **Affordability Challenges:**
- Growing concern about housing affordability in many urban centers, leading to increased interest in affordable housing solutions.
- Investors exploring opportunities to participate in affordable housing initiatives.

3. **Sustainability and ESG Focus:**
   - Rising importance of Environmental, Social, and Governance (ESG) criteria in real estate investment decisions.
   - Increasing demand for sustainable and energy-efficient properties.

4. **Flexibility in Lease Models:**
- A trend towards more flexible lease terms, including short-term rentals, co-living arrangements, and furnished rentals.
- Tenant preferences for flexibility in response to lifestyle changes and uncertainties.

5. **PropTech Integration:**
- Continued integration of PropTech solutions for property management, tenant engagement, and data analytics.
 - Increased reliance on technology for streamlined operations and enhanced tenant experiences.

6. **Economic and Policy Influences:**
- Economic factors, such as interest rates and inflation, influencing property values and investment strategies.
- Government policies impacting real estate markets, including incentives for development and changes in tax regulations.

7. **Community-Driven Development:**
- A focus on community-driven development with an emphasis on mixed-use spaces, walkability, and local amenities.
- Investment strategies aligning with community development goals for long-term sustainability.

8. **Adaptation to Demographic Shifts**:
- Consideration of demographic shifts, such as the aging population and the preferences of younger generations, in property investment strategies.
- Tailoring property offerings to meet the diverse needs of different demographic groups.

9. **Data-Driven Decision Making:**
   - Growing reliance on data analytics for investment decisions, market analysis, and risk assessment.
   - Integration of big data and predictive analytics to identify trends and opportunities.

10. **Alternative Investment Models:**
 - Exploration of alternative investment models, including real estate crowdfunding and Real Estate Investment Trusts (REITs).
 - Diversification strategies to minimize risk and optimize returns.

11. **Health and Wellness Considerations:**
   - Increasing consideration of health and wellness aspects in property design and amenities.
   - Properties designed to promote physical and mental well-being.

12. **Rise of Single-Family Rentals:**

- A trend towards increased interest in single-family rental homes, driven by lifestyle preferences and the desire for more space.
- Investors targeting single-family properties for rental income and potential appreciation.

Staying informed about these evolving market trends is essential for real estate investors to make informed decisions, adapt to changing conditions, and position themselves for success in dynamic markets.

Conclusion

Rental property investing remains a dynamic and resilient avenue for wealth accumulation and financial growth. As market trends evolve, investors should adapt to emerging opportunities and challenges. Embracing technological innovations, such as PropTech solutions and data analytics, enhances operational efficiency and tenant satisfaction. Strategic considerations, including diversified portfolios, sustainable investments, and attention to community-driven development, contribute to long-term success. Moreover, the impact of remote work, changing demographics, and a focus on affordability emphasizes the importance of staying attuned to shifting market dynamics. By learning from challenges, leveraging tax planning strategies like 1031 Exchanges, and integrating smart investment practices, investors can navigate the complexities of the real estate landscape and build a robust portfolio that stands the test of time.

1. **Diversification:**
- Spread investments across different property types and locations to mitigate risks associated with localized market fluctuations.

2. **Technology Integration:**
- Embrace technological innovations, including smart home features, PropTech solutions, and data analytics, to enhance property management and tenant experiences.

3. **Adaptive Exit Strategies:**
- Regularly reassess and adapt exit strategies based on economic factors, market trends, and evolving financial goals.

4. **Tax Planning:**
- Leverage tax planning tools, such as 1031 Exchanges, to defer capital gains taxes and optimize financial returns.

5. **Strategic Renovations:**
- Undertake strategic renovations to increase property value, attract quality tenants, and maximize rental income.

6. **Tenant-Centric Approach:**
- Prioritize tenant satisfaction by offering attractive amenities, flexible lease terms, and responsive property management services.

7. **Market Research and Analysis:**
- Conduct thorough market research to identify trends, assess property values, and make data-driven investment decisions.

8. **Sustainable Investing:**
- Consider sustainable and green investments, aligning with the growing demand for environmentally conscious properties.

9. **Risk Management:**
- Implement effective risk management practices, including understanding market trends, maintaining a conservative approach to financing, and establishing emergency funds.

10. **Continuous Learning:**
- Stay informed about evolving market trends, regulatory changes, and emerging technologies to adapt to the dynamic real estate landscape.

By incorporating these key strategies into their approach, rental property investors can navigate challenges, capitalize on opportunities, and build a resilient and profitable real estate portfolio over the long term.

Encouragement for Aspiring Investors

For aspiring investors entering the realm of rental property, your journey holds immense potential for financial growth and personal achievement. Here's some encouragement to guide you along the way:

1. **Educate Yourself:**
- Never underestimate the power of knowledge. Continuously educate yourself on real estate trends, market dynamics, and investment strategies. Attend workshops, read books, and stay informed about industry innovations.

2. **Start Small, Dream Big:**
- Begin your investment journey with manageable steps. Starting small allows you to learn and grow without overwhelming yourself. As your confidence and experience increase, you can aim for more significant opportunities.

3. Learn from Others' Experiences:
- Seek guidance from seasoned investors. Learn from their successes and, equally importantly, from their challenges. Real-life experiences are invaluable lessons that can shape your approach and decision-making.

4. Build a Strong Network:
- Connect with fellow investors, real estate professionals, and mentors. A supportive network provides insights, advice, and potential collaboration opportunities. Surround yourself with individuals who share your passion for real estate.

5. Embrace Challenges as Learning Opportunities:
- Challenges are an inherent part of any investment journey. Instead of fearing them, view challenges as opportunities to learn and grow. Each obstacle you overcome will contribute to your resilience and expertise.

6. Set Clear Goals:
- Define your investment goals early on. Whether it's building a passive income stream, achieving financial independence, or creating a diversified portfolio, having clear objectives will guide your decisions and keep you focused.

7. Be Patient and Persistent:
- Realize that success in real estate investing often takes time. Be patient, stay persistent, and don't be discouraged by initial setbacks. The long-term rewards are often well worth the effort and dedication.

8. Risk Management is Key:
- While real estate can be lucrative, it involves risks. Develop effective risk management strategies, conduct thorough due diligence, and make informed decisions to minimize potential pitfalls.

9. Celebrate Milestones:
- Acknowledge and celebrate your achievements along the way, no matter how small. Celebrating milestones provides motivation and reinforces your commitment to the journey.

10. Adaptability is Your Strength:
- The real estate landscape evolves, and the ability to adapt is crucial. Stay flexible, embrace change, and be open to exploring new opportunities and strategies.

Remember, every successful investor started as a beginner. Your willingness to learn, coupled with determination and strategic thinking, will pave the way for a rewarding and fulfilling journey in rental property investing. Dream big, stay focused, and enjoy the exciting adventure ahead!